Meet the ANGELS

Text by Léonie and Stratford Caldecott

Drawings by David Clayton

ResSource

Second Spring Catechesis

MEET THE ANGELS is published by ResSource Ltd in the UK, and distributed in North America by the Thomas More College of Liberal Arts (Second Spring Books).

6a King Street, Oxford OX2 6DF, UK
www.ressource.co.uk

The Thomas More College of Liberal Arts
MERRIMACK, NEW HAMPSHIRE • ROME, ITALY

Thomas More College, Six Manchester Street,
Merrimack, NH 03054, USA
www.thomasmorecollege.edu

All rights reserved. Text © Léonie and Stratford Caldecott.
Illustrations © David Clayton.
Printed in the UK by Joshua Horgan Print Partnership, Oxford.

ISBN: 978-0-9555380-2-5

THE INVISIBLE WORLD

The world is full of things we can't see. We can't see the wind, although we can feel it. We can't see gravity, or magnetism, but they are real. We can't see love, but it is the most important thing in the world. We can't see God.

We can't usually see angels either. Angels are God's spiritual friends and messengers. He can see them, because he knows everything without needing eyes. He knows the angels because he made them: he made them even before he made us.

Some people think of an angel as being like a fairy that we put at the top of the Christmas tree. That's OK if you remember the angel is a messenger from God, like the star that guided the Wise Men from the East to find the baby Jesus in Bethlehem. But an angel is not a fairy. An angel is an awesome spiritual being who lives close to God, loving and praising him night and day. Each of us has a special angel of our own: our Guardian Angel, sent by God to guide and protect us through our life.

Of course, angels don't need to be noticed. They *like* being invisible. It doesn't stop them helping us, or helping God. So you don't have to notice them, but it is nice to know they are there. They are devoted to Jesus, and they do whatever he asks of them. They are so pure that they can see God all the time, because the pure in heart can see God. As you color in this book, pray to become as pure as the angels. In your own way, you too can be one of God's messengers to the world.

CHOIRS OF HEAVEN

"Where were you when I laid the foundations of the earth, when the morning stars sang together, and all the sons of God shouted for joy?"

The angels are God's children. They sang with him when the world was made. There are thousands upon thousands of angels. Each of them is different from the others. The Bible tells us about them.

The Seraphim, Cherubim and Thrones are the angels closest to God. The ones called Dominions, Virtues and Powers are a bit lower. Then come the Principalities, Archangels and "ordinary" angels. Our picture shows Jesus in the middle of all these angels.

The highest of all angels, the Seraphim, see God face to face, loving and praising him. They are sometimes shown as looking like fire, meaning the fire of God's eternal love. They are described by the Prophet Isaiah as having six wings. *"With two he covered his face, and with two he covered his feet, and with two he flew."*

The Cherubim appeared to the Prophets to look like a Man in the front, an Eagle from behind, a Lion if you approach from one side, and a Bull or Ox if you approach from the other.

The angels called "Thrones" are pictured supporting God's throne in heaven, and to the Prophets they looked like great spinning wheels, or wheels within wheels, "full of eyes" because they can see into all things. (You will find a picture of them with the Seraphim and Cherubim at the end of the book.)

INVISIBLE FRIENDS

You have a friend.

Every one of us has a Guardian Angel to guide and protect us. This invisible friend helps us to pray, reminds us what is the right thing to do, and protects us if we pay attention to him. He stays with us from the beginning of our life to the end. He is like a shepherd for our souls, leading us closer to God.

One day the Apostle Peter was in Herod's prison when an angel appeared to him and made the chains fall from his hands. The guards fell into a deep sleep, the prison gates opened mysteriously, and the angel led him out of the prison and set him free. Then he disappeared.

You can speak to your Guardian Angel, as you can to the other angels you will meet in this book, and to the human saints as well. You can speak to them in your heart, quietly and privately, so no one else can hear. You are never really alone, and never without a friend, even if you cannot see him.

Jesus told his followers about our angels: *I tell you that in heaven their angels always behold the face of my Father who is in heaven* (Matthew 18:10). An angel is always with us and with God at the same time.

Night prayer to the Guardian Angel
Angel of God, my guardian dear,
To whom God's love commits me here,
Ever this night be at my side,
To light and guard, to rule and guide.
Amen

ENTERTAINING ANGELS

Sometimes an angel can appear like an ordinary person. We can meet them and not know who they are. That happened to our ancestor Abraham.

A long time ago, God made a covenant – a special kind of promise – to an old man called Abraham. He said that if he would worship God faithfully, he would give him many children and his descendants would live in the Promised Land.

Soon after that, three mysterious men came out the desert to Abraham's tent. He knew there was something special about them: maybe he thought they were angels.

Abraham and his wife Sarah made them a meal, but Sarah laughed when they said she was going to have a baby, because she was an old woman. But later this came true, and Sarah gave birth to Isaac. God can make anything happen.

Abraham was speaking with the Lord God when he was speaking to the mysterious men. God's messengers bring us closer to God, and God is always in them. They do what God wants, and they say what he says, because they love him.

STAIRWAY TO HEAVEN

Abraham's grandson, Jacob, was to be the father of all the tribes of Israel. Just before he met his future wife, he was travelling through the countryside as it became dark. He lay down to sleep with a stone for a pillow.

In the night he had a dream. He dreamed that there was a ladder like a stairway standing on the earth, and its top reached up all the way to heaven. Jacob could see the angels going up and down between earth and heaven.

At the top, above the ladder in his dream, he could see God. And God said, "I am the Lord, the God of Abraham. I will give the land to your descendants, and I will look after you wherever you go."

Jacob woke up amazed. "The Lord is here, and I did not know it," he said. "This is the house of God, and the gate of heaven." He made a pillar out of the stone he had slept on, and dedicated it to God. Jacob's ladder or stairway reminds us of the way to heaven, the way that the angels take all the time.

TOBIAS SEARCHES FOR LOVE

A young man called Tobias (another descendant of Abraham) came from a very poor family. His father, who was blind, wanted him to get married, and so he sent him on a journey to ask for some money that was owed to the family, and to find a wife.

Tobias took his dog along, and also a young man he had just met who called himself Azarias. His real name, though, was Raphael and he was an archangel in disguise, sent by God to help the boy.

One of the things Raphael did was help him catch a big fish. Later, at the end of their journey, Raphael introduced him to a young woman called Sarah, who was sensible, brave and beautiful, and Tobias fell in love with her. But he was afraid to marry her, because she had been married seven times already and each time her husband had died on the wedding day!

Raphael showed Tobias how to burn part of the fish to drive away the devil that had been killing all the other men, and then Raphael tied him up so that Tobias and Sarah could get married safely.

After they were happily married, Tobias, Sarah, Raphael and the dog went back to Tobias's father, who by this time was very worried about him. Raphael used part of the fish to heal the old man's eyes. When he could see again, he was so happy, he threw his arms around Tobias and Sarah. Then Raphael explained who he really was.

This is part of a prayer Sarah's mother said when she knew the couple were safe:

Blessed are you, O God, with every pure and holy blessing.
Let your saints and all your creatures bless you;
Let all your angels and your chosen people bless you for ever.

ANIMALS AND ANGELS

Animals are often very close to angels. In the Old Testament book of Numbers, we are told the story of Balaam, who was famous for cursing people. A king called Balak was afraid of the people of Israel, the descendants of Abraham, so he asked Balaam to come to him and put a curse on Israel.

On the way to Balak, Balaam was riding a donkey, and the donkey saw an angel of God in the road, standing with a drawn sword, so the donkey stopped and would go no further. Balaam could not see the angel and he was so cross with the donkey that he beat her with a stick. But she lay down on the ground and still wouldn't budge.

When Balaam beat her again, God allowed the donkey to speak, and she said, *"Why are you beating me? Don't you know I have always been faithful to you?"*
And then Balaam saw the angel at last, and the angel praised the donkey for saving Balaam's life (because if she had gone on walking, he would have had to kill him).

The angel told him to go to Balak but only to say the words he would tell him to say. So Balaam did, and instead of cursing Israel in the ceremony, he ended up blessing and praising Israel instead. *"Blessed be every one who blesses you, and cursed be every one who curses you,"* he said to Israel.

God protects his people when people hate them, and his angels are always at work, even when we cannot see them (but sometimes when we can't, maybe the animals can)!

WHO ARE THE ARCHANGELS?

Angels were made free, just like us. Like Adam and Eve in the Garden of Eden, they had to choose how to behave. Some of them chose to reject God's love, and to live for themselves alone. For that reason, they could no longer be with God and live in heaven forever. Where they went to instead is called hell. Their leader was once an archangel called Lucifer. Now he is called the Devil.

Heaven and hell are real, but they are not in the sky or under the earth. You can only get to them by being like them: either filled with God's love, or filled with hate. The person who loves and does what God wants is filled with light, and has nothing to fear. The angels are stronger than the devils.

Raphael and Gabriel are both archangels. And leader of the armies of heaven is the Archangel Michael, who is always protecting us. You can say this special prayer to him whenever you feel worried or frightened.

Prayer to St Michael
Saint Michael the Archangel, defend us in battle.
Be our defence against the wickedness and snares of the Devil.
May God rebuke him, we humbly pray,
and do thou, O Prince of the heavenly hosts,
by the power of God, thrust into hell Satan,
and all the evil spirits, who prowl about the world
seeking the ruin of souls. *Amen*

MARY'S YES

Mary was a young Jewish girl who lived in a town called Nazareth and was about to be married to a good man called Joseph. Mary was kind and gentle, and she was looking forward to being married to Joseph. But then something strange happened.

An angel appeared to her – it was the Archangel Gabriel – and said, "Hail, full of grace! The Lord is with you." She was surprised to see the angel, and to hear him say these things, but Gabriel told her not to be afraid, because God loved her very much.

Gabriel told her that even before she was properly married to Joseph she would become pregnant with Jesus, the Son of God, through a miracle. Jesus would later be king over all the people, and he would rule forever. He would be the Son of God.

But it all depended on her saying "yes". Even though she didn't understand how this was going to happen, she told the angel that she would do whatever God wanted. *"Behold, I am the handmaid of the Lord. Let it all happen as you say."*

The angel went away, and Jesus began to grow in Mary's womb. She went to tell the good news to her old cousin, Elizabeth, who was soon to be the mother of John the Baptist. But she didn't know what to tell Joseph!

Luckily, she didn't have to tell him anything, because the angel appeared to Joseph in a dream with a message. God still wanted Joseph to marry Mary in order to look after her and the baby. He wanted Joseph to call the baby Jesus, which means THE ONE WHO SAVES.

Hail Mary, full of grace,
the Lord is with thee.
Blessed art thou among women
and blessed is the fruit of thy womb, Jesus.
Holy Mary, mother of God,
pray for us sinners now and at the hour of our death.

CHRISTMAS ANGELS

Jesus was not born at home in Nazareth, but in the little town of Bethlehem, where Joseph's family came from. Joseph and Mary had to go there because the Roman government wanted everyone to be registered in the town their family came from. Lots of people had to do the same thing, so Bethlehem was very crowded, and even though Mary told Joseph the baby was about to come, they could not find anywhere comfortable to stay. So when Jesus was born, they had to put him in a manger that was full of straw for the animals.

Meanwhile, out in the fields that night there were shepherds, looking after their flocks of sheep. Suddenly an angel appeared to them and the sky was full of light.

They were terrified, but the angel said, *"Be not afraid; for behold, I bring you good news of a great joy which will come to all the people."* And he told them that Christ the Lord had been born. Then thousands of other angels appeared, singing *"Glory to God in the highest, and on earth peace among men with whom he is pleased."*

When the angels had disappeared back to heaven, the shepherds went to find Mary and Joseph and the baby lying in a manger, and told them what they had seen and heard.

JESUS IN THE DESERT

A bad king wanted to kill the baby Jesus because he had heard that when he grew up he would be a king too, but the angels warned Joseph in a dream to take Jesus and Mary away to a safe place.

So Jesus was kept safe by his parents, and when he grew up his Father in heaven told him he was ready to teach the people how to love God. Jesus went to be baptized by his cousin John in the river, and when he came out of the water the Holy Spirit appeared to him. The Spirit looked like a dove, and led him into the desert places where the animals lived, to prepare him for what he must do.

For forty whole days he did not eat anything at all, and then when he was very hungry the Devil appeared and tempted him to use his power to turn the stones into bread. But Jesus would not do what the Devil wanted him to do, only what his Father in heaven wanted. Next the Devil said Jesus should ask the angels to carry him into the air. That would make everyone listen to him. When he would not do that either, the Devil said Jesus could rule the world if he just agreed to worship the Devil instead of God. Again, Jesus refused.

Jesus showed us how to say no to temptation and yes to God. And as soon as he had sent the Devil packing, angels came and looked after him in the desert.

COMFORTED BY AN ANGEL

The angels helped Jesus later, too. Three years later, when a lot of men were planning to kill him, he went to pray to his Father in the garden of Gethsemane at the Mount of Olives. He knew he would have to die, but it was a terrible thing to have to face. The idea of suffering like that seemed to him like a great cup of bitter medicine that he would have to drink in order for us to get better.

As he prayed, an angel from heaven came to make him feel a bit stronger. The angel comforted him the way angels try to comfort us, too, when we are afraid.

His disciples were not able to pray with him or help him, because they were too sleepy. Jesus would have felt all alone, if the angel had not come to him.

JESUS DIES FOR US

They did kill Jesus. They arrested him, and accused him of things he had not done, and then they nailed him on a Cross and left him to die.

He could have saved himself, but he didn't, because he wanted to save us instead. By dying like that, he was able to go into the world of death, and rescue all the souls who loved God. He was able to build a road from death into heaven.

But it was a horrible way to die, and especially because he had not done anything wrong. All he had done was love people, and teach them to love God, and to love each other. He had told the truth, and he had healed people from sickness.

Most of his followers, except his mother, Mary Magdalen and a young disciple called John, had run away. There were crowds of people staring at him as he died. But the angels were there too, sorrowing and worshipping. They understood what was happening. Angels can help us to understand things that make us sad and puzzled.

A Prayer to Jesus on the Cross
Lord Jesus, crucified for us,
in the presence of Mary our Mother and the holy angels
I want to thank you for saving me.
Fill my heart with grace, so that
I may receive the gift of everlasting life
and see your Glory with the Father and the Holy Spirit.
Amen

THE PROMISE OF LIFE

The body of Jesus was put in a tomb with a great rock across the entrance. But on the third day after his death, when his disciple Mary Magdalen and some of the others came to see it, the rock had been moved and the body was no longer there. Inside the tomb they met two angels who looked like young men in dazzling white robes, sitting where the body had been.

The women cried because they thought someone had stolen the body, but the angels told them not to be afraid. They said that Jesus had risen from the dead, as he had promised he would, and was alive again! The women ran to tell Peter and John and the others, but they could hardly believe the story, it was so amazing.

When they came back to the tomb, they found out it was true. The tomb was empty. Then Jesus himself met Mary Magdalen in the garden, and comforted her. He told her he was soon going to go back to heaven to be with his Father. But before that he visited the other disciples, so that they would believe what the angels and the women had said.

Jesus has conquered death! He is alive and will never die again. We too, after we die, will meet Jesus and will live forever with him and the angels.

MARY QUEEN OF ANGELS

Jesus loved his mother Mary very much. When her time on earth was coming to an end, the disciples all gathered around in sorrow to say goodbye. But her body was taken up to heaven by the angels, where her Son gave her the new life that we will all receive one day.

He did more than that: because she was his beautiful mother, who had given him everything and brought him up when he was on earth, and because his Father loved her just as much as he did, he crowned her *Queen of the Universe*, and made her Queen over all the angels.

Mary still lives in heaven. She is like a mother for the whole world, and she prays for us all the time. Sometimes she visits the earth, sometimes with her angels, and many children and saints have seen her. She always tells them to be good and to love one another, and to pray as much as they can to God. She gave us the Rosary to help us to pray.

The picture shows Mary surrounded by her angels and holding the baby Jesus. It is based on a famous painting called the Wilton Diptych, and it shows the way one of the Kings of England, Richard II, liked to think of her, when he wanted to give his kingdom to her and her Son.

WHERE TO FIND THESE STORIES IN THE BIBLE

Choirs of Heaven – Colossians 1:16, Ephesians 1:21, Ezekiel 1:5-21, Isaiah 6:1-3.

Invisible Friends – Acts 12:1-19. *Catechism of the Catholic Church*, paras 328-36

Entertaining Angels – Genesis 17:1-8, 18:1-15.

Stairway to Heaven – Genesis 28:10-22.

Tobias Searches for Love – Book of Tobit, with prayer from Tobit 8:15.

Animals and Angels – Numbers 22:1 to 24:25.

Who are the Archangels? – Revelation 12:7-9

Mary's Yes – Luke 1:26-38; Matthew 1:18-25.

Christmas Angels – Luke 2:1-20.

Jesus in the Desert – Matthew 3:13-4:11.

Comforted by an Angel – Luke 22:39-46.

Jesus Dies for Us – John 19:17-30.

The Promise of Life – John 20:1-23.
Luke 23:54-24:53.